DIPLODOCUS

Written and Illustrated by

Michael W. Skrepnick

GIGANTIC LONG-NECKED DINOSAUR

Enslow Elementary, an imprint of Enslow Publishers, Inc.

Enslow Elementary® is a registered trademark of Enslow Publishers, Inc.

Copyright © 2005 by Enslow Publishers, Inc.

Library of Congress Cataloging-in-Publication Data

Skrepnick, Michael William.
   Diplodocus—gigantic long-necked dinosaur / Michael W. Skrepnick.
      p. cm. — (I like dinosaurs!)
   Includes bibliographical references and index.
   ISBN 0-7660-2622-1
   1. Diplodocus—Juvenile literature. I. Title.
   QE862.S3S484 2005
   567.913—dc22
                           2004016787

Printed in the United States of America

10 9 8 7 6 5 4 3 2 1

Series Literacy Consultant:

Allan A. De Fina, Ph.D.
Past President of the New Jersey Reading Association
Professor, Department of Literacy Education
New Jersey City University

Science Consultant:

Philip J. Currie, Ph.D.
Curator of Dinosaur Research
Royal Tyrrell Museum
Alberta, Canada

Illustration Credits: Michael W. Skrepnick

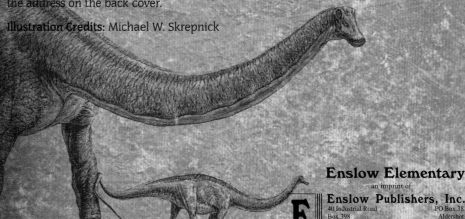

Enslow Elementary
an imprint of
Enslow Publishers, Inc.

E

40 Industrial Road
Box 398
Berkeley Heights, NJ 07922
USA

PO Box 38
Aldershot
Hants GU12 6BP
UK

http://www.enslow.com

CONTENTS

WORDS TO KNOW

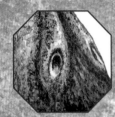 nostrils (NAH strihlz)—A pair of nose holes used for breathing.

 predators (PRED uh tur)—Animals that hunt other animals for food.

 skull—Bones that make up a head.

MEET DIPLODOCUS (dih PLAH doh kus)

Diplodocus ate only plants. It raked in juicy green leaves with dull, flat teeth. Its wide jaws chomped down plants . . . all . . . day . . . long.

LONG-NECKED DINOSAURS

Diplodocus belonged to a group of huge, heavy dinosaurs. They all had very long necks, and many had even longer tails.

They had to eat plants all day to feed
their huge bodies.

HOW BIG WAS DIPLODOCUS?

Baby *Diplodocus* started life in an egg. The egg was a bit smaller than a basketball. When *Diplodocus* hatched, it was the size of a small dog.

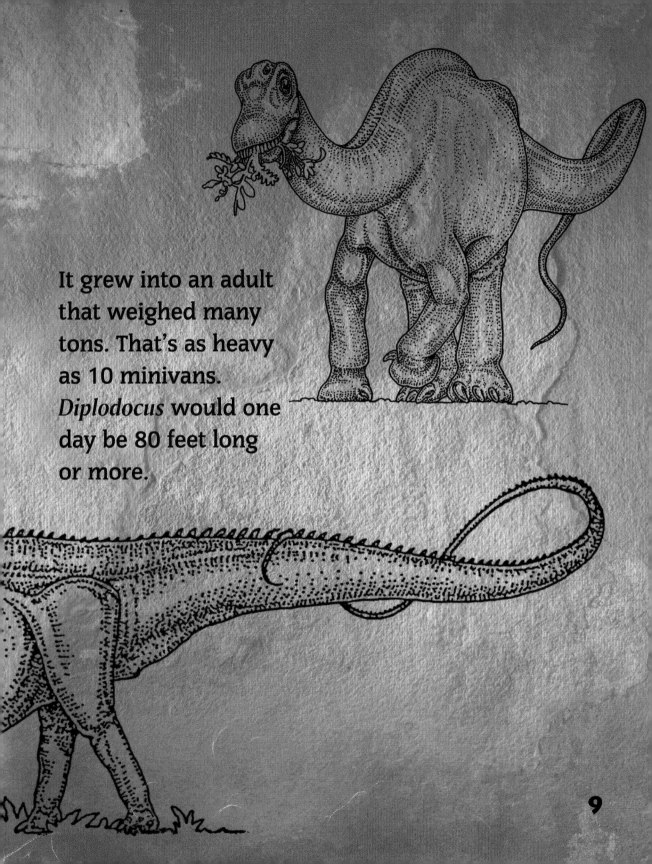

It grew into an adult that weighed many tons. That's as heavy as 10 minivans. *Diplodocus* would one day be 80 feet long or more.

SAFETY IN NUMBERS

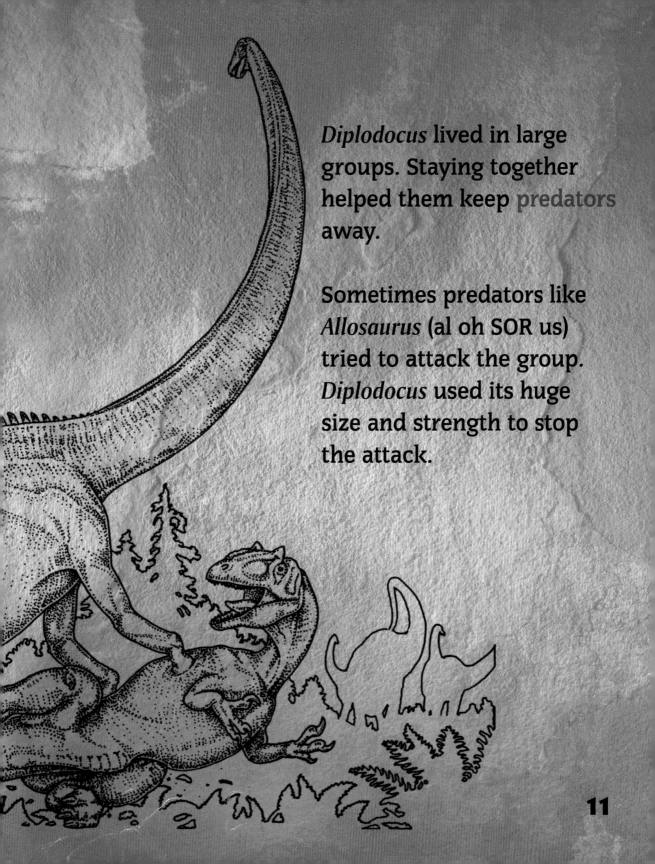

Diplodocus lived in large groups. Staying together helped them keep predators away.

Sometimes predators like *Allosaurus* (al oh SOR us) tried to attack the group. *Diplodocus* used its huge size and strength to stop the attack.

DIPLODOCUS' NOSE

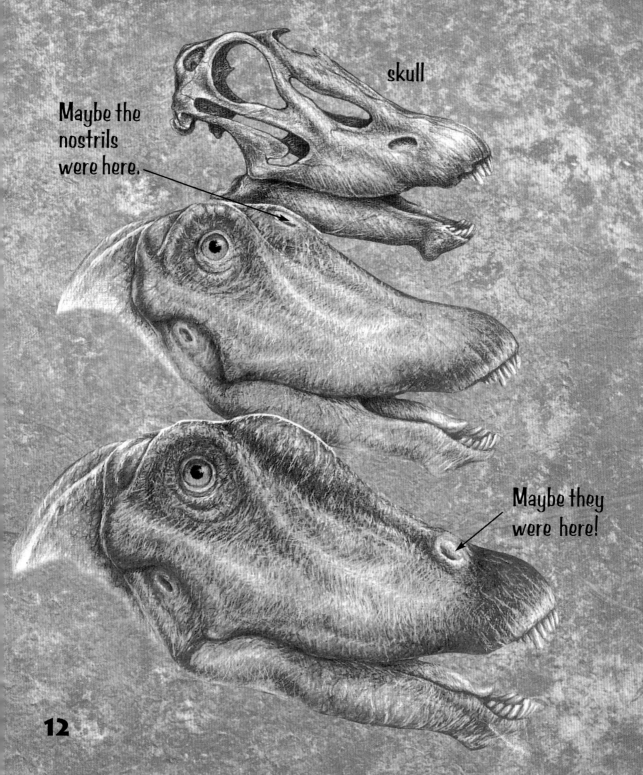

skull

Maybe the nostrils were here.

Maybe they were here!

Can you guess where *Diplodocus'* nose was?

Its skull had a large hole on top, so the nostrils might have been right on top like a whale's.

But maybe they were further down on the face. Scientists are not sure yet. They are studying the skull for more clues.

PLANT EATERS

Diplodocus held its head and neck close to the ground. It had to, because it ate short plants.

Other kinds of long-necked dinosaurs held their heads and necks high off the ground. They ate leaves from the tops of tall trees.

MEET BRACHIOSAURUS

Diplodocus was just one kind of long-necked dinosaur. Another was *Brachiosaurus* (BRAK ee oh sor us). You could feel the ground THUMP when *Brachiosaurus* slowly marched by.

Its long front legs and long neck made it look like a giant giraffe. With its head held so high, *Brachiosaurus* could see food and predators from very far away.

17

ENEMIES

Long-necked dinosaurs ate only plants. Other dinosaurs ate only meat, including the meat on other dinosaurs!

T. rex hunted *Alamosaurus*, another long-necked dinosaur. What a battle! *T. rex* ripped into *Alamosaurus*'s side. *Alamosaurus* fought back.

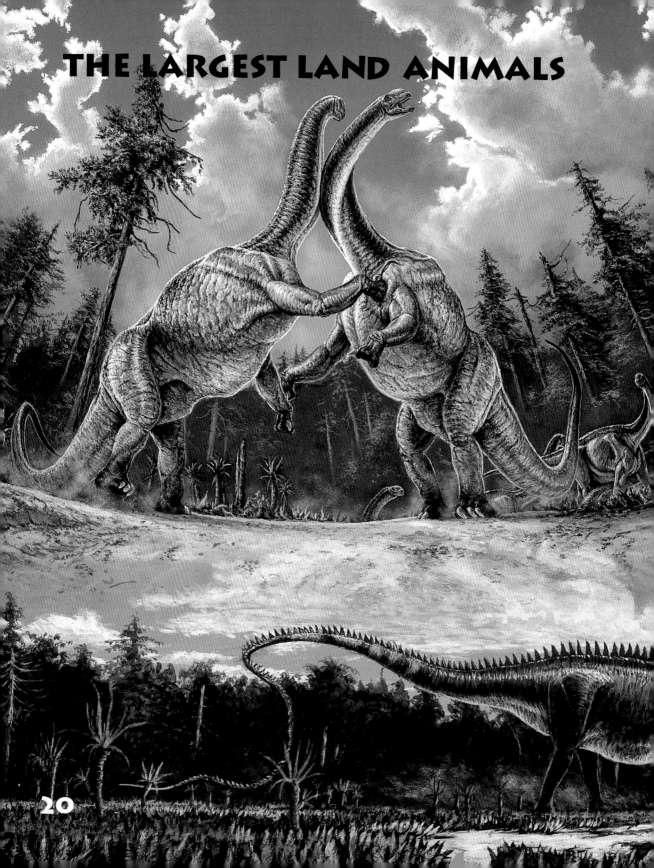

THE LARGEST LAND ANIMALS

Diplodocus and the other long-necked dinosaurs were the largest land animals ever to have lived. Sometimes they battled each other. Who would be the strongest and be the leader of the group?

Only their bones are left to help us learn about these dinosaur giants . . . and a time when their footsteps shook the earth.

DIPLODOCUS FACTS

- *Diplodocus* could not bend its neck very far from side to side.

- *Diplodocus* may have cracked its tail like a whip.

- *Diplodocus* may have had pointy spines on its back.

- *Diplodocus* swallowed stones to help its stomach mash up food.

- *Diplodocus* had only one claw on each hand.

LEARN MORE

BOOKS

Dodson, Peter. *An Alphabet of Dinosaurs*. New York: Scholastic Inc., 1995.

Lessem, Don. *Scholastic Dinosaurs A to Z: The Ultimate Dinosaur Encyclopedia*. New York: Scholastic, Inc., 2003.

Thomson, Ruth. *Dinosaur's Day*. London: DK Publishing, Inc., 2000.

Williams, Judith. *Discovering Dinosaurs with a Fossil Hunter*. Berkeley Heights, N.J.: Enslow Publishers, Inc., 2004.

WEB SITES

The Children's Museum of Indianapolis
<http://www.childrensmuseum.org/kinetosaur/index.html>

Discovery Kids
<http://kids.discovery.com/fansites/prehistoric/prehistoric.html>

National Geographic Kids
<http://www.nationalgeographic.com/ngkids/0005/dino/>

INDEX

About the Author

Michael W. Skrepnick is an award-winning dinosaur artist. His artwork is featured in many natural history museums and appears in scientific journals, books, and magazines. Michael lives and works in Alberta, Canada, close to some of the richest deposits of late Cretaceous dinosaur fossils in the world.

Note to Parents and Teachers: The I LIKE DINOSAURS! series supports the National Science Education Standards for K–4 science. The Words to Know section introduces subject-specific vocabulary words, including pronunciation and definitions. Early readers may need help with these new words.